LONG LIVE OUR FREEDOM

The Author

Tarisai Chendambuya was born on 20th June 1974 in Makoni District. He grew up and attended several schools before completing Ordinary Level in 1990 and Advanced Level in 1992.

He holds a Bachelor of Science (Honours) Degree in Police and Security Studies from Bindura University of Science Education in addition to other certificates. He is married to Priscillar Mamhunze and has three daughters.

LONG LIVE OUR REVOLUTION

Some people are born revolutionaries, some become revolutionaries, some, join and find themselves swept along by the revolution. Some people are born enemies of the revolution, some become enemies of the revolution, some, join enemies of the revolution and find themselves swept along by enmity to the revolution.
This sums up the protagonists of a revolution.

Revolutionaries are everywhere, in the same manner as there are enemies of the revolution everywhere. They are born every day, the same as enemies of the revolution are conceived and born every day. You have revolutionaries at all levels of society and you have enemies of the revolution at all strata of society.

The revolution is born of itself. Its glowing ambers simply invite the revolutionary to shove in logs and blow tirelessly and relentlessly into them. The revolutionary's objective is to raise temperatures until his rival run out of ideas on how to bring the temperatures down. If ever anyone tells you, no matter how repeated, that he or she started a revolution, that's a lie.

It has and will always be the greatest iron of many, if not all, revolutions that the revolutionary become a candidate for charges of both moral and criminal subversion of the revolution. Some become candidates for posthumous charges of palpable connivance in the subversion of a people's revolution. All their graveside speeches become eulogies crudely painted and decorated by an orgy of sentimental hypocrisy.

Through the revolutionary's acts of both commission and omission, the revolution become a huge monument standing, no longer by itself, on high moral ground that require unsolicited moralizing. The revolution turns the revolutionary into a hypocrite when it becomes a land afflicted by a perpetual cosmic diarrhea, when it becomes a monument, a world heritage site sitting lonely on top of the tallest mountain in the land earning nobody money.

Instead of the revolution remaining a rallying point, it becomes an excuse for a revolutionary to indulge in his appetite. It self-relegates from being a people's revolution to a revolutionary's revolution. This degenerate relationship between the revolutionary and the revolution is a red flag.

Owning and defending the revolution for its own sake is counter-revolutionary. It topples the revolutionary from high moral summits into the deep valleys beyond the animal kingdom. Such ownership and defense buries, into the mud, the very people the revolution seeks or seeked to raise from the dust.

When the communal ownership of a revolution is only used as a giant metaphorical condom by the revolutionary, it loses its appeal in the eyes of the people whose conscience will have retained its virginity. The revolution loses its moral significance and become, literary, a war. Everything else becomes consequences of war because war inevitably has consequences.

A revolution is a gentleman in a pure revolutionary sense and in the strict dictionary meaning of the original word gentleman. Once a revolution assumes the meaning of the word gentleman as used along Chinoyi Street and Mbare Musika, the revolution ceases to be a revolution in the sense we would have ordinarily wanted it to remain.

While a revolution perpetually evolves, the wars which may accompany the revolution should become a closed chapter. If violence and murders, both psychological and physical, remain or become top of the arsenals by which the revolutionary defend and sustain the revolution, then the revolution loses its meaning and value. The colour of the lenses, through which ordinary citizens see the revolution and the revolutionary, become blood red.

During the struggle that is the revolution, the revolutionary chants to the struggling masses, 'THE STRUGGLE CONINUES'. When the end of the most vicious part of the struggle culminates in the clothing of a nation in new independence gabs, the struggle to sustain and defend the revolution should continue without the masses continuously struggling in a war with no end in sight. If this does not happen, the masses lose faith in the revolution and future struggles for emancipation and empowerment.

When the revolutionary returns home, from the revolutionary struggle, without the main object of the revolution but new guns and war planes alone, the revolution will struggle to shed off the tag of a wasted effort. It does not make the revolutionary's credentials any more colorful than they were before when he starts raving and ranting, reminding the masses that he was cheated on behalf of the masses into accepting a less than half victory. Future generations will really need to shut their eyes, ears and minds to reason if the revolutionary struggle is to retain the same moral significance as at when the nation got independence.

You see, revolutionary struggles kill and maim people. This is fact. However, where the masses perceive themselves as enjoying holiday on a hijacked ship at high seas, those who laid their lives and limbs for the revolution become merely reminders of the consequences of participating in a war. Their genuine case and sacrifice fails to sustain the moral fiber that usually weaves and fire a revolution. It, alone, smacks of hypocrisy as a justification for the treatment of the masses at the hands of the revolutionary who would have hijacked his own ship.

The revolution is a journey with a purpose in which the end justifies the means and the means moralize the end. How the revolutionary trudges the few kilometers before the destination places both the revolution and the revolutionary under the microscope when it becomes clear to the masses that independence was achieved with some unfinished revolutionary business.

When the revolutionary opens the doors to the revolutionary museum and shows you to the room of unfinished revolutionary business but does not want you to proceed to the room of why there is a room full of unfinished revolutionary business, you ask WHY? It is when the revolutionary climbs on top of the tallest mountain in the land the following morning, and shouts 'THE STRUGGLE CONTINUES' that you begin to have a glimpse of WHY. The revolutionary will now be sitting in a different chair putting on a different suit.

The woman who marries does not remain just a woman. She becomes something else, a married woman. The set of rules that she used to fight women's wars get modified as she adjusts to fighting the same wars as a married woman. She becomes a liability to the fight of the true woman. The same happens when the revolutionary takes off the revolutionary jacket and puts on that of a President or Prime Minister in office. Its simple fact, where he used to fight with you, he now rules you. Where the office of the revolutionary fights with you, the office of the president fights you and rule you. The revolutionary cannot put on the office jacket of president of an independent country without risking comprising the revolutionary jacket.

When the woman marries and bears children, it is hypocrisy of the highest order for her to go back to her constituency and claim she has had children, the natural way, without losing her virginity. Even in the absence of children, it still is hypocrisy to claim that she is enjoying sex without losing her virginity. The least it can be, without being offensive, is it's a plain lie.

Reasonably, it is very difficult for a revolutionary's conscience to retain its virginity after it has had sexual intercourse with an official office as the presidency of a country. The true revolutionary should never occupy such office. That office has completely different eating habits to those of the revolution. The true revolutionary's dietary laws are driven by selflessness whilst those of an official presidency are underpinned by charity of the jungle, of the animal kingdom.

A true revolutionary has one character and face whose colours are a reflection of the power of the people and by the people. When the revolutionary assume the official presidency of the country, his character and face become chameleonic. Colours reflect the powerlessness of the masses.

During the revolutionary struggle, the revolutionary army is loyal to the interests of the masses. It undergoes an ideological metamorphosis of unimaginable proportions when it puts on the new jacket of a national armed forces and become loyal to the rulers of the day. Loyalty to the masses become relative. A red flag flies on the top of the tallest building in the capital city. It signals the last post and bon voyage to the true revolution.

Very long stories can be written about the revolution. Cities, roads and streets can be named in the name of the revolution. These become merely reminders of a chapter in a country's beleaguered history which must be ignored as soon as the bus passes them. The revolutionary struggle becomes an unfortunate victim of subsequent chapters. These chapters would have served one purpose only, to wipe away any emotional attachment to the preceding chapters. To a country's lasting agony, the subsequent chapters do not write themselves and the revolution suffers when authors of the subsequent chapters include the revolutionary.

When the post-independence chapters become scribbled in red, those of the masses who have the revolution stuck in the gut of their conscience become victims of an emotional crisis. They do not know whether to hate or like the revolutionary anymore. They are not sure on how to deal with or save the revolution stranded between the massive jaws of a colourless alligator. That shows you the extent of the good that a people's revolutionary efforts would have brought them.

When the revolutionary turn into a sullen cop manning a permanent roadblock and the revolution become a permanent roadblock, liberation theory and liberation politics ceases to direct independence and empowerment. Something else, more counterrevolutionary, takes over, deceit and self-centeredness. This is the reason why politicians are the worst thieves, fraudsters and murderers ever to walk on two feet. Yet this is our daily bread and dilemma.

When the revolution is dragged through the mud right to the podium of excuses, it self-relegates to just another topic for inclusion in the ordinary level examination syllabus. When it is defended in a cocoon of deceit and self-centeredness, it gets stripped of any semblance of moral validity.

When the masses want to defend the revolution, in earnest, they find that the revolution would have already become indefensible elsewhere. The people should now speak but literally mind their mouths lest they fall foul of the revolutionaries in office. What dies then is not the revolutionary but the revolution. What loses significance more is the revolution and revolutionary effort and not the revolutionary.

The revolution is greater than the revolutionary.

Long live our peace.
Long live our freedom.
Long live our independence.
Long live our revolution.
Long live our true revolutionaries.

WISHES AND POSSIBILITIES

Imagine it or not. Talk of terrifying contradictions.

From the darkest depths of your conscience comes the rays of light that brighten up the wishes of a generation and extinguishes the future of another. Such is the usefulness and uselessness of a people's history.

Do not mind whether this is an American disease or some European plague. Neither should it be your concern whether this is an African disaster or an Asian catastrophe. They all have a dark pit in their conscience from which come rays of light that brighten up the wishes of a generation and extinguishes the future of another. This is neither a masculine or feminine phenomenon. It however does assume masculine savagery and feminine generosity and affection. This is what makes the human component the most dangerous and yet most important of all components that make up and participate in world, continental and domestic politics.

The human being is the world's only hope for salvation. He is also the worst nightmare barrier to salvation. The United Nations was created by human beings, politicians, for the good of all nations. It was and has been destroyed and rendered useless by human beings, politicians. The United Nations gave hope to many but has succeeded in taking away the hopes of so many.

World leaders and leaders of countries, small and large, developed and developing, grew powerful and resolved conflicts. They have gone on to saw the seeds for the next conflict. When they go to solve a war, they identify all the possible means and ways to stop the war. They also identify all the possible means and ways by which they can make money out of the war and their efforts to stop the war, even creating another war.

We thus say in Shona then, '*hand yemunhu munhu.*" This means a person's enemy is a fellow human being. I am still wondering how and why the greatest threat to family peace is your father and his brothers when they start fighting over the family chieftainship. There is an unrelenting stalker to a country's peace.

Quite a number of events or a series of events have pestered my mind and shape my views of Zimbabwean politics in general and party politics in particular. There has always been inter and intra party violence since the days of the liberation struggle for Zimbabwe's independence, to the general elections in 1980, 1985,1990, 1995, 2000, 2002, 2005 up to when violence reached epic proportions during the harmonized elections of June 2008.

The problem is that the generality of the citizenry has hopelessly continued to hope that politicians and political education will solve the question of violence. Interestingly violence has continued to dog Zimbabwean politics because the cause lies elsewhere and it is fueled by the selfishness of mankind which gives birth to the use of and perpetration of violence.

You see, I learnt during my days in the police that to reduce the risk of a thief breaking into your motor vehicle, you only had to remove valuables like expensive cell-phones, laptops, jewellery and money from the vehicle. At one time a female officer joked that, "Remove the vagina from the woman and you eliminate rape." She then sarcastically added that because the male species is brutish and selfish, he would divert his unlawful canal pursuits to the female species of animals like dogs, chicken, cows, goats and donkeys just to quench his satanic canal longing and lust.

This point, made in jest then, now became relevant as one tries to think how else can we deal with or remove a large percentage of violence in Zimbabwean politics. The question become, how can we remove the vagina from the woman and stop the man from continuing it with or on dogs and chicken. The crux of the headache is, we must definitely remove the vagina and at the same time make it very difficult for the man to indulge in his appetite even with dogs and chicken. This should, at the same time, have the long term effect of empowering the generality of our people politically, economically and socially.

It kind of tires the soul and deflates the spirit when everybody speaks against violence and prays for peace but you wake up the following morning and the first thing to greet you is a horror story of lost limbs and life from political violence. You begin to wonder whether you were praying for an escalation of violence.

The questions that continue bugging you are countless. They have always been bugging and begging for an answer. Why is there a break-down of the rule of law when it comes to issues relating to politically motivated violence? Why are we always accusing the police of selective enforcement of the law in such issues? Where do perpetrators of political violence get the courage and will to indulge in their activities? Where will be the police when perpetrators of political violence go about their business? What makes the police or army to be so ineffective in dealing with political violence?

The thing is, when political violence and killings happen, the assumption is it is members of the public beating each other, burning down each other's houses and killing each other. The question is then, how does a national police force and army fail to stem this madness?

You also wonder why do members of the public themselves indulge in this madness of politically motivated beatings and killings? Why do political leaders fail to stop their supporters from beating, maiming and killing their opponent's supporters? How do political leaders manage to persuade men and women, neighbours and friends to beat, maim and kill each other in the name of their country? Why and how do the people or supporters themselves agree or find it reasonable to beat, maim and kill fellow human beings in politically motivated violence? What is their motivation?

All of us may have all the answers to these questions but in most cases these are outward manifestations of the underlying cause. The same cause why Idi Amin had friends and supporters at home and abroad. When you see the cause you will begin to understand why there has always been political violence in Egypt, Iran, Ivory Coast, Senegal, Zimbabwe, Myanmar, Mexico and many other countries the world over.

Party politics is public enemy number two after the people in politics.

Party politics came to Zimbabwe with colonialism. The objective is not to blame colonialism for bringing the concept of party politics to Africa. That one is a tired line of excuses. Party politics gave birth to parties like NDP, ZAPU, ZANU, ZANU (PF), MDC and the rest of the chain of MDCs and other part timers.

Basically a political party is a grouping of people who share a common political ideology and interests. They have a common way of pursuing their interests for the mutual benefit of party functionaries. The party name and symbols become merely rallying paraphernalia. The experience in Zimbabwe show that the degree to which anyone can benefit from the party association depends with the level at which one is serving the party. The bottom line is there is some element of beneficiating that keeps the party spirit burning. What then is cultivated is the 'what is in it for me mentality', never mind the noises about patriotism and sovereignty. Party functionaries are patriotic to the political party and work to protect its sovereignty.

When the party wins an election, experience has shown that the party systematically rewards the brave, the hardworkers and collaborators. Therein lies the biggest problem and weakness of party politics. Through the use of enabling and friendly legislation, it is not difficult to reward party functionaries after winning an election.
Take note that the rewarding is done after winning the election.

The president gets elected on a party ticket. He picks his cabinet or ministers from the members of parliament of his political party who are in parliament on a party ticket and therefore gets their ministerial appointment on a party ticket. You do not have to be loyal to the country to be a minister, you have to be very loyal to the political party.

All the ambassadors who end up representing their country in foreign countries are appointed from the party. They are party functionaries. These people are loyal to the party first and to the country last. The other side of the story is, you don't have to be very loyal to the country to be an ambassador but you need to be very loyal to the political party, never mind the noises about patriotism, sovereignty and people first speeches.

Ministers and their deputies including the permanent secretaries and directors of various departments within ministries are appointed directly and indirectly through the party. Included among directors are commanders of the uniformed forces. The umbilical cord that attaches them to the commander- in- chief and political party is never severed by the noises of the need to be apolitical, whatever the good intentions of the word. The fact remains that they are appointed from the party, never mind the cosmetic appointment process in the constitution which is designed to disguise the reality of the appointment.

The Attorney General, who is literally the top judicial officer and supposed to ensure that your aggressor is subjected to justice, is appointed from the party, indirectly though. Do not worry about the wires surrounding his office to distance him from the party. Do not get lost in the network of drains, in the constitution, leading to his appointment, they wind and weave back to the president and party.

The Supreme Court bench and High Court is made up of highly decorated law-men and women no doubt. However this band of learned men and women come from the same cave as the Attorney General and commanders of the uniformed forces. The road network to their appointments follows the same curves and terrain.

Provincial Governors, Administrators and District Administrators come from the party. They are appointed directly and indirectly from the party.

When party policies manifests themselves as national policies, party functionaries benefit more from them than any other citizen. The extent to which you can benefit depends on your position in the party and the perceived-level of contribution towards ensuring that the top leadership attains the positions that they desire. You must be visible to the leadership otherwise you will remain honored as a mere party cadre carrying a cherished vote from which no benefit accrue.

The foregoing is just but a micro glimpse of how party politics exploits the beneficiating factor in literally making party functionaries, up to the party president, chase the proverbial hare with salt in their pockets.

It is this system, party politics, which ensures an unrelenting supply of green cards to the school of political violence. The animal instinct to gain and control from a platform of political victory is fired by party politics. In the world of party politics the end justifies the means, and if it means killing or maiming so be it. After the victory, the victor can always afford to say 'we' are sorry or it was unfortunate, 'we' should put the past behind 'us', whatever it requires to place oneself on high moral ground.

It is this system that places or pits us against our neighbors. It turns your son against my father and me against your brother. We kill each other because we are aware of what we stand to gain or lose if our parties win or lose, not because we love our country. That is a plain lie. The end justifies the means.

It is this God forsaken system that turns the uniformed forces from their jobs and against themselves. It explains why a well-equipped army, whose excellence and exuberance is always paraded for all to see it's mighty, fails to stop 'mere civilians' from killing and maiming each other in political violence or 'for the love of their country'. It also explains why a well trained and equipped police, whose reputation for competency in law and order is etched in the histories of so many countries the world over, fails to stem political violence in their own backyard

It explains why prisons are full of all transgressors of a country's laws except perpetrators of political violence. The few that manage to window-dress the criminal justice system are sufficient motivation for the remaining majority to remain convinced that the few are merely the cost and minimum risk of doing business.

It explains why all political leaders and their supporters are always victims of political violence and never perpetrators of political violence. It betrays why political leaders, when preaching peace, use peace verses pregnant with violence endorsing commentary. They know that, should violence propel them to power, they have the rewards and penalties in their hands.

Party politics, by breeding self-seeking party functionaries aiming to gain from a political victory, secured by whatever means, will ensure that the sword remains the ultimate arbiter for years if not generations to come. Until we unseat party politics and especially the beneficiation factor together with the capacity of a victor to reward those who used violence to propel him or her to the throne, political violence is here to stay. We will have to rely on the selflessness of man to unseat the selfishness in the midst of our politics.

Terrifying though is the possibility that a country born out of the selflessness of man can be devoured by the selfishness of man unless the selfish self-seeking are unseated and we make it very difficult for politicians to reward their supporters.

BEHIND A NATION'S PROBLEMS

There are men and women out there, very dangerous men and women. It is scurry when they stand before you as your leaders. It is worse when you realize that when you see the head of a scorpion coming out of a hole, what is trailing behind is the stinger and you have nothing in your armory to stop the scorpion from coming out.

When they decide to lead us they say they are our messiahs and yet, like the earth's crust they float on a time bomb, on an ocean of molten rage, a sea of bubbling boiling and rumbling magma which is often under so much pressure it, when an opening is forced to present itself, bursts forth through the crust of our lives in a torrential shower of violent, vicious and fatal destruction.

Where a country, perpetually, remain seated on such crust because of the scorpion syndrome, the inhabitants will never know peace. The question has been, is right now and will always be, for how long will the people brave the eruptions with apparent resignation? Yes, the human spirit might be irrepressible but will social, economic and particularly political volcanoes ever become extinct? Have we not seen these things relentlessly shower us with carefree abandon, us the helpless islanders, with creeping boiling death, glowing ash and lava?

When these things, politicians, politics and political violence threatened to engulf Zimbabwe in and around

June 2008, our hearts wept uncontrollably. It was and still is this world where you try to scream but no sound come out. You try to lift a finger but nothing works. You blink your eyes and frown, still nothing works. It is like you are talking to nobody, listening to nobody and seeing nobody. You want to play a part but you are helpless, caught in the paralyzing grip of society's anesthetics.

You are dipped in questions that you can't answer. Such questions as, do we need clean murder or dirty murder? Are certain weapons of death no worse than others of mass destruction and do we need any that are sneakier or no sneakier in manner of delivery than the unseen firing of lethal explosives from vast distances away?

It is funny but comically nonsensical. The opposition accuses ruling party politicians and the ruling party politicians counter-accuses the opposition politicians of possessing simple-and-cheap-to-make weapons whose lethal possibilities are terrifying. They accuse each other daily of acquiring ballistic missiles that can be used to drop poison on enemies hundreds of miles away in the communal lands. To them accumulating supporters is like stockpiling deadly weapons, *makona,* whose manufacture is easily concealed and protected by law. They are weapons to use against each other, kill and maim each other in the name of their country.

A lot of questions have remained unanswered. You can't ask politicians or anybody religiously involved with them, politicians. You can't ask a group of men who can't bring themselves to ask why addicts die from overdoses even after their bodies have grown used to the drug in question, men who you find to be blind enough not to see or feel anything when the whole country stand trembling, salivating and wetting our pants when we suddenly found ourselves in deep waters of political violence, hands tied on our backs. They do not care how we have continued to hallucinate and hiss at imagined tormentors, paralyzed with perpetual fear of what they are planning or dreaming next.

It leaves one's mind option less but depending on one's subjective or objective perspective, unchaining these chained slaves of their nature, their upbringing, our upbringing and their subsequent lives can be a moral victory, for the abused and our innocent culture and intelligence or a defeat for their science and medicine. Such unchaining should not be regarded as a passing fancy but a principled attempt to redefine some of our basic concepts about the nature of our cultural, social and moral rights and obligations.

The road from independence and the stretch before it has taught us that politicians do not miss an opportunity to move mountains from where the eye enjoyed them most if it will put or keep them in political office. When this becomes their main objective, any diversification is sure delving deeper and wide from spook nursing to manning graveyards and sleeping in deep, dark uninhabitable alleys. At this point of their carriers, they all make one disastrous mistake of finding value in vice. All their friends, at home and abroad, become just but a hideous clique, one of the so many across continents who are vexing things, distorting culture and creating culture valueless ness.

When political office becomes the politician's main thrust of policy, the politician is the answer as to why giving a man authority without responsibility encourages irresponsibility in him and resentment in the peaceful populace. The electorate becomes the answer as to why it is equally catastrophic to saddle a man with responsibility but to give him no authority thereby extinguishing his value.

Politicians, especially their conscience, die when the pursuit of political office becomes the main inspiration to policy and choices of how to implement policy. They eliminate, from their conscience, questions such as what does it take for a man to behead an innocent man and can anyone object, on what grounds, ethical or theological? You begin to wonder, if not, men should be taught that all their mischief employed, rejection will definitely follow and ensure we will remember them for all the wrong reasons than would have been the case without such deployment.

When you can't complain about them without risking being killed or maimed by one of them, the country is alive but the nation is dead. It becomes gold to know and always remember that when adults breathe through their anuses, God gave you the nose so that you can keep the mouth shut. This becomes so because politicians try to make you very aware that the mosquito that buzzes the loudest and descend to within earshot gets squashed first. This is why many of the kindest and wisest people in most set-ups remain ball watchers from the sidelines. The truth is that they can score high on selfless ness and dedication than most of the politicians who masquerade as nurses, doctors, counselors, commentators and panelists working to cure the cancer that has and will continue to eat us all away.

The rules of secrecy, strict observance and identification with the politician's agenda, which the politician enforces on everybody becomes a psychologically violent and murderous enforcement of previously non-existent laws against a degenerate myth. The politician indoctrinates and converts the most ardent of his followers   into mythical creatures divorced from normalcy and reality. Give them any sought of stick and they will invariably seize it by the wrong end, mistaking cannibal autocratic authority for patriotism and vulgar nationalism for sovereignty, condoning gratuitous persecution of innocent and peace loving souls who thought they had rights.

The blood of innocent people tastes sweetly as collateral damage on a politician's tongue.

A politician pursuing his own agenda has a very defective machine to feel with and his thinking just reflects this status-quo.

The forces of darkness descend upon the whole country when politicians start playing this game of removing taste buds from the tongues of their conscience in pursuit of political office. Unfortunately this game of harnessing diabolical supernatural powers, which combine evil with brutality and use obscure rules in a crude game of graveyard wrestling and underworld force, in its obscurity, elevates itself to national virtue status.

At the height of political careless ness, the electorate becomes merely an uneasy host of critics, looking on and huddled in the way of disaster and muttering, each to themselves. That is when others begin to realize that, in this ball game, you had to have a big body so that you can be held up before the small boys as a superior being. The careless politician, at the apex of political careless ness, believes he has more right to life than any of you. His agenda has more right to existence and success than any of us has ever been given by God and the Universal Declaration of Human Rights.

At the summit of political careless ness, no one can tell the leader to stop burning the chicken run together with the chicken or throw away the baby together with the water. Even some of his followers are forced into a wounded hostility against their own leader but when the leader speaks they, like everybody else, smile wryly at it. They are afraid to tell their leader that his favorite techniques have a lot of head-butting, eye-gauging and testicle-squeezing. Neither can they tell him that all the vigor and erotic enthusiasm that he feels when boot meets teeth or knee meets groin in pursuit of his agenda, will one day end leaving radioactive remnants which will hound the country for generations.

Politicians, at the deepest end of uninhibited political careless ness, have no mercy in their cupboard of morals. They deliberately cripple everything and everyone by pushing sharpened bicycle spokes into the neck vertebrae. Such satanic stern ness reduces everyone, including some of the most competent citizens to involuntary quadriplegics.
A country may have problems but a careless political leader is the real superior menace, an emotional and moral outrage, which reduces the rest of the citizenry to inferior people who are unable to get on even with legal discrimination which protects citizens from their leaders and politicians.

When problems elsewhere threaten to swallow the politician, he identifies enemies from within and without. How they choose to deal with perceived enemies and gain or regain political ground has often converted an area of formerly outstanding natural beauty to an environmental outrage. More often than not, the destruction is almost irreparable and takes generations to be reversed, not even by a team of gardeners who have achieved exactly the right balance between neatness and disarray.

Political careless ness bears the same characteristics as general sinning. It, like women, often becomes more masculine with age, growing beards and going bold, while, like old men, it sometimes grow saggy middle-aged breasts. This is why when they decide to talk of what is and what has gone wrong, their talk rarely gets past the obvious and when it does, it sometimes veer towards the dubious. Every one of them is right. Each time they open their mouths, they behave like they have something to hide, typical of the behaviour '*yemunhu akaromba*' and you are left wondering what evolutionary psychology have to do with such behaviour except to show that the politician is an ape who, even though evolution took place, has never been fully adapted to walking on flat ground.

The bottom line is, there is no solution to a country's problems or future to its off-spring for as long as politicians pursue political office to beyond the point of diminishing responsibility.

VICTIMS

When all is said and done, the victim is buried and the mass grave starts to grow green, soft, grass. Our assessment of his innocence matters no more than an ordinary layman's psychiatric assessment of a street beggar.

After that you can only look and cry endlessly. Questions linger on, who did what? Who permitted what? Who is at fault? If no one, then what is wrong? If both, who shoulders the largest potion?

It may be unsound but victims have always blamed the son for doing and equally the father, relatives and countrymen (us) and everyone else for picking their teeth while the son makes sure every family member's tail remain stranded between the hind legs.

When the victim is buried, victims remain here and beyond the grave. Political violence has victims here, in the grave and beyond the grave. The victim of political violence remain, perpetually, in a situation in which he is more like an emotionally desperate teenager who has no family, friends or neighbors.

You wonder if, at some point or stage, it becomes the only remaining remedy to chop off a man's feet to make him short so that you remain the tallest in the land. If this is so, then it surely raises a lot of questions about our culture.

Did we inherit a doctored culture? If that is so, did the doctoring gave rise to a problem? Were it or these a direct result of habitual negligence or a result of deliberately perverting a previously sound culture? Who doctored the culture?

In trying to answer these questions, the victim ends up feeling merely deafened by history and future's roar. Everything shows towards a culture in search of meaning and redefinition to the victim. His only comfort is that whatever good bits remain of our culture is the citadel we must defend and the stage on which we must triumph. The victim would think, as he watch chicken rejoicing in harmony through the open door, 'blessed are the chicken of this land for they can still afford to share a husband without a fight while humans are in a world in which it is no longer common for a neighbor to borrow a cup of sugar without risking death.'

When the victim retires to bed, he sees nothing but the roof, hands behind the back of his head. From the roof, questions come down to him. Does securing practical and theoretical benefits for one's family automatically justifies experimentation on other fellow men? Can this justify feeding pesticides and bombarding them with radiation until they lay bleeding from the mouth and anus? How about confining your own children, brothers and sisters in a well of evil despair until lasting psychological damage make them wear a permanent smile that turn them more into grinning robots? Have not our minds, in the name of politics, grown more vicious to the extent of telling us, 'It is not enough to kill, go on and degrade the body. It is dead with two knife wounds but take an axe and chop it to pieces to send the right message'? Are we not also bound to be killed in these psychotic rages or murdered in the course of our endeavors to feed our habits?

The victim wonders, if not, we are creatures saddled by God with all goodness but are practically more interested in ripping each other's clothes off than anything else. It is only in his bedroom that the victim can skin alive the perpetrator of his misery. Beyond the bedroom he realizes the perpetrator is more like a sexual demon whose lust would relegate ancient Babylon, Sodom and Gomorra to the rank of meek forgivables. Unlike Sodom and Gomorra, they can kill you for sexual pleasure for that is their ego, their life, carriers and dreams.

The victim knows that careless politicians have a train-like ego, ominously large, deceptively fast and too slow to stop. They are, in the criminal enterprise, the only mafia bosses who do not realize that they are running a criminal enterprise in the name of representing the people's wishes. You ask them to draw the line on unethical, barbaric and corrupt behaviour, they always oblige but make sure to always write it in pencil.

The victim, looking at the roof, realizes that the careless politician lie and lie until his audience no-longer recall what really it is that he was lying about. They do not care that it is their careless ness that send the victim's brother to his grave. They enjoy their carriers the same as they enjoy their sex. They are dirty men whose moral and social fiber has been ravaged, plundered and destroyed by the drive and temptation of their political carriers. These men and women who have a cynical belief that they alone are the savers of mankind and any situation when arguably they have been the worst destroyers of mankind because their political carriers are more precious than your life.

They are the reason why Sudan has not known peace, the alter on which Hutus and Tutsis were sacrificed, the reason why the Americans are the worst peace reverends, the God forsaken uterus that gave us mankind buggers like Hitler and Mussolini, daring cannibals like Idi Amin and Betrand Bokassa. They are the peace of hell and sanctuary of firebirds, the spine of swines, lubricant of Somalia's hunger famine and deaths and perpetual despiser of Somali and Sudanese women's beauty.

When victims are moping their tears and struggling to raise funds for memorials of their unfortunate relatives, themselves victims of senseless politics, perpetrators will be readying themselves for a Bill Clinton. You remember him, the American President, running away from hurricane Lewinsky and cyclone Paula to find comfort in Africa, comforting skulls, bones, skeletons and graves, the unforgettable archives of Rwanda, to prop up his political standing in our shamed but shameless eyes, licking Rwandese tears and kissing headless Tutsi corpses before rushing to ride elephants in Bechuanaland. To the victim they are all writers of Lucifer's bible and manners of a United Nations of disjointed nations.

The victim blames himself for being a victim, a coward and thinks of fellow victims as lovers of their cowardice and enjoyers of a stability and continuity of life inextricably tied up with a kind of tragic innocence and naïve ignorance, dashers of their own wishes well-rehearsed in the weather.

Victims cry out to no one because no one hears them when the proverbial elephant and hypo collides on the road to political office. They cannot hear the victim because their thinking becomes orgasm after orgasm. The victim has no place to hide when perpetrators decide to use problems to solve a problem and fight genocide with genocide. It is these sexual demons who elevate meanness to a virtue in parliament and walks out on peace because she is not their type of lass.

All the victims' cries become one. You can only cry to yourselves, "Oh God, see us here at the mercy of the ones who never give others a fair chance nor their women rest or peace. They would rather lick you dry and still want to squeeze a little bit more out of you."

The victim has no choice but to accept that this is a type of men who have a greater supply of male hormones that causes them to have much stronger sex urges than the normal male and are seemingly less able to resist the ugliness of sex, men who have been hell-blessed with oceans and Himalayas of testosterone. They would make you want to know if our behaviour is influenced by fundamental biologically corrupt mechanisms which may well go beyond heredity. You would want to ask what is it that predisposed the human race in particular to become so anxious, restless, careless and cold calculating.

The victim thinks then that political carelessness is a cynical accomplishment in which virtually no learning is involved at all. Looking at the roof of his bedroom, the victim realizes that those who ride to political office on our deaths are convinced we are like chimpanzees, animals with no natural language of our own but can be emotionally aroused to speak and use one of their choice. That is why they find it easy to tell everyone through a newspaper that the death of a victim's brother from their random fire was collateral damage and yet these perpetrators are users of self-brewed-up multifarious disasters to scare the wits out of us inhabitants of the gutter.

The victim knows he will know no peace as long there is another election to come and all politicians think they should rule you, with or without your mandate. The electorate knows that when politicians think political violence, in whatever form, guarantees one's ticket to political office, such politicians are the wrong means and very wrong partners necessary for implementation of a culture of peace and harmony. He realizes helplessly that these people are nothing but angels of horror and hollowness who fan ethno-nationalism, xenophobia, racism, discrimination, practice and encourages religious extremism and violations of poor men's rights. They are cruel persecutors of genuine asylum seekers, refugees and immigrants. They can enjoy watching the victim rotting in the gutter as long they attain political office and influence. They distrust, they suspect, they have no tolerance, hurt and hate, quell, kill, are sick and seek more sickness, dirty and yet clamor for more dirt, are incoherently nasty but think nasty is a virtue and not nasty by itself.

These killers, promoters and advocates of war and death are the devil's autocratic firebrand cannibals who derive pride in denying the tramp his pride of place in the alley, alien animals from an alien ravine whose human tails are kept wagging by waging an alien war on humanity's conscience. If the tramp is not careful, he will be eaten no matter how dirty. If the mad man strays onto their dinner tables, they will make him into chops and steaks and munch him with garlic and chilies.

To the victim, one innocent death, because brothers are skirmishing for political office, is horrible, it is terrible, no, horrid horrifying holocaust unto itself. Yet, to these men and women, it is collateral damage that must be forgotten. Such type of persons are, to the victim, the ultimate undoing of human endurance, men who have had an unappeased, irresistible and insatiable drive for more and more horror bestowed unto them by the devil. They are tigers who move around the world, in very long robes, planting bombs on all foundations of freedom, justice and peace, even in the name of the firebrand angel democracy. They talk of peace as if peace could be raised at a Mayor's Christmas Cheer Fund, these hypocrites who send their problems abroad to preach peace and settle disputes while at home they are in arms races and militarization. They are the damn rogues who had the cunning audacity to rig the election that would have brought God to power at the United Nations, telling the inhabitants of the gutter that cultural diversity was a hybrid parrot species of cultural adversity.

As he retires to bed, the victim holds a silent prayer, a threat to invade heaven, words of the last cries of an angry destitute from a hole in the countryside.

"God, I would not say I have been here for too long though you have kept me here unnecessarily for too long. I would not like to tempt your appetite for throwing us at the mercy of the devil's savage appetite to indulge in his appetite. The fires in hell hold the key but if I can summon all destitutes of my courage, we could destroy heaven in an avalange of destitution and overrun hell in one gutsy effort to mortify our flesh and withstand punishment here and above. You see these people you put here do not think a destitute has a right to food which must not be denied by policy makers in the name of so called economic realism. This is sensible crying I am directing at you as my maker. The segregatory policies here on earth are devoid of destitute concern and have led not only to civil disturbances in urban areas but also desolation in the countryside. They do not care that what is perceived as a moral imperative may, tomorrow, become a political necessity. They think solutions are found just in offices and laboratories and do not know that a destitute's illiteracy does not mean ignorance any more than their knowledge means wisdom. God, please God, these privileged few and the very few need to be reminded that the poor have legitimate aspirations to a better life and peace in our holes on your earth. Their careless assumption that if the rains fail, as they have done in recent years, less food will be grown and destitutes will inevitably starve is, as per your permission, a mere comfortable bedroom abdication of any responsibility for our destitution, the same way a predecessor will always remain some kind of alibi.

They flood and plug our countryside holes saying destitutes are a threat to stability and we say heaven we come. These people will wait until an ultimate crisis of destitution and desperation has brought the destitutes a voice which, no matter how disorganized, is able to impose itself on their conscience. This voice, heavens, we have been denied. Instead heavens, you have imposed on us a bunch of people whose criticism of what has gone wrong carries with it the assumption that they alone can equally put things well again, people who are quick to use the weather as an excuse to cover failures of policy, careless even if that does not validate the enormous damage they would have done to us destitutes. Heaven why are you allowing them to use the destitute until he becomes a land unable to meet the demands of decent destitution put upon it by morality? God, these crooks who will die catering to the aspirations of the urbanites for their tables to remain full, they think destitutes are lazy forgetting that the destitute are more likely to remain huddled, unprotected, in disaster's way because they can't afford to be anywhere else. One day destitution is going to kill us and bring us there in large numbers than heaven can handle and hell can cremate, never mind the bible."

The victim fall asleep, not sure if ever he will know real peace

www.ingramcontent.com/pod-product-compliance
Lightning Source LLC
Chambersburg PA
CBHW071018290526
45795CB00005B/1850